RELEASED FROM CIRCULA....

W9-COM-778

J296 PEN

WAYNE PUBLIC LIBRARY
3737 S. WAYNE ROAD
WAYNE, MI 48184-1697
734-721-7832

SEP - - 1998

Discovering Religions

JUDAISM

Sue Penney

RSVP

RAINTREE
STECK-VAUGHN
PUBLISHERS
The Steck-Vaughn Company

Austin, Texas

Text © Sue Penney 1997.

All rights reserved. No part of this book may be reproduced or utilized in any form or by any means, electronic or mechanical, including photocopying, recording, or by any information storage and retrieval system, without permission in writing from the Publisher. Inquiries should be addressed to: Copyright Permissions, Steck-Vaughn Company, P.O. Box 26015, Austin, TX 78755.

Published by Raintree Steck-Vaughn Publishers, an imprint of Steck-Vaughn Company.

Library of Congress Cataloging-in-Publication Data

   Penney, Sue.
   Judaism / Sue Penney.
      p. cm. — (Discovering religions)
   Includes index.
   ISBN 0-8172-4393-3
      1. Judaism—Juvenile literature.   I. Title.   II. Series.
   BM573.P46 1997
   296—dc20   96-33727
                                                         CIP

Religious Studies consultant: W. Owen Cole and Steven L. Ware (Drew University)

Thanks are due to Rabbi Douglas Charing, Rabbi Arye Forta, and Rabbi Steven Kushner for reading and advising on the manuscript.

The author and publishers would also like to thank Rabbi Arye Forta for his help with the translations of scriptures.

Designed by Visual Image
Typeset by Tom Fenton Studio
Cover design by Amy Atkinson
Printed in Great Britain

1 2 3 4 5 6 7 8 9 WO 99 98 97 96

Acknowledgments

The author and publishers would like to thank the following for permission to use photographs:

Cover photograph by Juliette Soester.

The Ancient Art and Architecture Collection p. 39; Werner Braun pp. 40 (top), 42 (top), 44; J. Allan Cash Photo Library p. 32; Circa Photo Library pp. 12, 17; Bruce Coleman Ltd. p. 25; A. H. Edwards/Circa Photo Library p. 13; Robert Harding pp. 6, 38; The Hutchinson Library p. 16; Jewish Education Bureau p. 8; The Jewish Museum p. 23; B Key/Christine Osborne Pictures p. 37; Peter Osborne p. 40 (below); Zev Radovan pp. 33, 34; Anat Rotem-Braun p. 21; Barrie Searle/Circa Photo Library pp. 11, 27, 29, 31; Juliette Soester pp. 10, 14, 18 (below), 28, 42 (below), 45, 47; The Weiner Library p. 36; Zefa pp. 7, 9, 15, 18 (top), 20, 22, 26, 46.

The author and publishers would like to thank the following for permission to use material for which they hold the copyright:

The Assembly of Rabbis of the Reform Synagogues of Great Britain for the extracts from Reform services on pages 17 and 45 and the Israeli Declaration of Independence on page 39, which were published in *Forms of Prayer for Jewish Worship I*, 7th edition, 1977; Dalia Hardof Renburg for the Hamantaschen recipe, on page 23, which was published in *The Complete Family Guide to Jewish Holidays*, Robson Books, 1987; JNF Publishing Co. for the Hebrew alphabet, on page 13; Clive A. Lawton for the Passover song, on page 27, which was published in *The Seder Handbook*, Central Jewish Lecture and Information Committee, The Board of Deputies of British Jews, 1984; Vallentine, Mitchell & Co. Ltd. for the extract from *The Diary of Anne Frank*, 1954, on page 37.

The publishers have made every effort to trace the copyright holders, but if they have inadvertently overlooked any, they will be pleased to make the necessary arrangements at the first opportunity.

3 9082 07253 5621

CONTENTS

MAP: WHERE THE MAIN RELIGIONS BEGAN

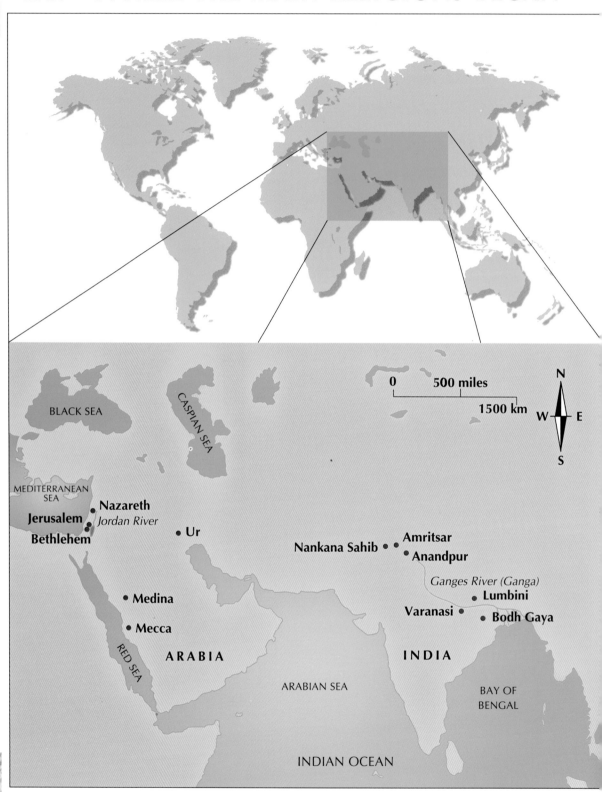

BLACK SEA

CASPIAN SEA

MEDITERRANEAN SEA

0   500 miles

1500 km

N
W   E
S

Nazareth
Jerusalem
Jordan River
Bethlehem

Ur

Nankana Sahib   Amritsar
Anandpur

Ganges River (Ganga)

Medina

Varanasi   Lumbini
Bodh Gaya

Mecca

RED SEA

ARABIA

INDIA

ARABIAN SEA

BAY OF BENGAL

INDIAN OCEAN

TIME CHART: WHEN THE MAIN RELIGIONS BEGAN

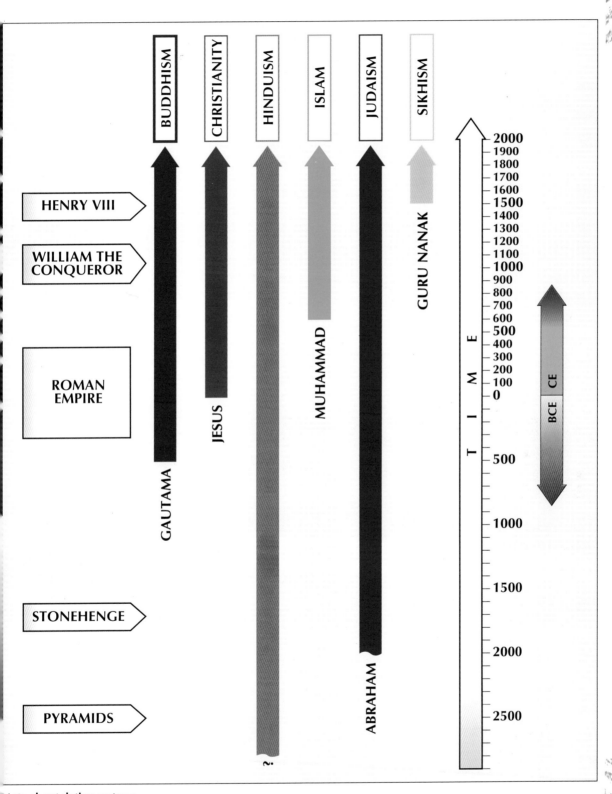

Note about dating systems

In this book dates are not called BC and AD which is the Christian dating system. The letters BCE and CE are used instead. BCE stands for Before the Common Era and CE stands for Common Era. BCE and CE can be used by people of all religions, Christians too. The year numbers are not changed.

INTRODUCING JUDAISM

This section tells you something about who Jews are.

The word "Jew" can be used in two ways. It means someone who was born a Jew. It also means a Jew who follows the Jewish religion, which is called **Judaism**. Not everyone who was born Jewish chooses to keep to the religion. Some people who were not born Jewish choose to become followers of Judaism. In this book, "Jew" means a follower of the religion of Judaism.

What do Jews believe?

Jews believe that there is only one God, who is **eternal**. This means that he was never born and will never die. He is always present everywhere, and he knows everything. He made everything, including the world and everything in it. He cares about everything that he made and he listens when people pray to him.

When Jews pray to God, they call him **Adonai**. This means Lord. Jews think that God's name is very important, so they use it with great respect. They never use it carelessly.

Jews do not believe that they are the only ones who know what God is like, but they do believe that Jews have a special relationship with God. They believe that God gave laws

This modern sculpture of a menorah is in Jerusalem.

The Star of David is on Israel's flag.

Temple was destroyed in 70 CE. It was the most important building in the Jewish religion.

The other symbol is a star with six points. This is called the Star of David, or sometimes the Shield of David. No one really knows where this symbol came from, but it has been used for hundreds of years. It is used as part of the flag of Israel, the country where many Jews live.

that they must obey. As long as they obey the laws, God will look after them. Their relationship with God is based on love. One of the prayers that Jews use most often shows how important this is. It says, "You must love the Lord your God with all your heart, with all your mind, and with all your strength." This prayer is called the **Shema**.

Jewish symbols

Jews use many **symbols** in their religion, but two are especially important. One is the **menorah**. It is a candlestick that has seven branches. It reminds Jews of the lamps that were used in the **Temple** in Jerusalem. The

NEW WORDS

Adonai Name for God (means Lord).
Eternal Lasting forever.
Judaism Jewish religion.
Menorah Seven-branched candlestick.
Shema Jewish prayer.
Symbol Something that has a special meaning, or stands for something else.
Temple Most important place of Jewish worship (destroyed 70 CE).

THE SHEMA

This is the first paragraph of the Shema.

> *Hear, Israel, the Lord is our God, the Lord is one. Now you must love the Lord your God with all your heart, and with all your soul, and with all your strength. And these words, which I am commanding you today, shall be upon your heart. And you shall teach them carefully to your children, and speak of them when you are sitting in your house, when you are walking along the road, when you lie down, and when you rise up. And you must bind them as a sign upon your arm, and they shall be a token between your eyes. And you must write them on the door posts of your house and on your gates.*

Deuteronomy 6 : 4–9

The Synagogue

This section is about the special place where Jews worship and the things you find there.

A **synagogue** is the building where Jews go to worship God. The building is also used as the place where Jewish children are taught about their religion and learn **Hebrew**. Hebrew is the language that the Jewish **Scriptures** are written in so it is important for Jews to understand it.

Inside a synagogue

The most important thing in a synagogue is the **Ark**. This is a special cabinet that is at the front of the main room. The **scrolls** are kept in the Ark. A scroll is like a book with one long page, which is unwound so that it can be read. The scrolls are very important because the **Torah** is written on them.

Inside a modern synagogue. (In some synagogues the women's section is separate.)

Scrolls

A scroll is a long roll made of pieces of **parchment** stitched together. Parchment is made from animal skin that has been dried and smoothed so that it can be written on. The scroll has a wooden roller at each end, which the parchment is wound around. A scroll is about 200 feet (60 m) long. Scrolls are written by hand, using special ink. The writing is in Hebrew. Scrolls are very important, so they are looked after very carefully. The parchment is never touched with the hands. When someone is reading from the scroll, a special pointer is used to follow the words.

Each scroll has a special cover that is used when it is put away in the Ark. The cover is called a **mantle**. It is usually made of silk or velvet. Mantles are often beautifully decorated with embroidery. Sometimes scrolls have other decorations, too. These are called the crown and bells. They help to remind people that the scrolls are important.

Other important parts of the synagogue

The eternal light

In front of the Ark is a lamp whose flame never goes out. This helps to remind people that God is always present. It also reminds Jews of the lamp that was in the Temple.

The Ark is at the front of the synagogue.

NEW WORDS

Ark Cabinet that contains the scrolls.
Bimah Platform the reading desk stands on.
Hebrew Jewish language.
Mantle Cover for scrolls.
Parchment Writing surface made of animal skin.
Scriptures Holy books.
Scroll Roll of parchment the Torah is written on.
Synagogue Jewish place of worship.
Torah Books of Teaching.

The bimah

In the front of the synagogue is a raised platform, which is called a **bimah**. The Torah is read from a table on this platform, and the person who is leading the service may stand there.

The women's section

In traditional synagogues, men and women do not sit together. Women have a separate section of their own.

THE IMPORTANCE OF THE TORAH

This story was told by Rabbi Jose, the son of Kisma. It shows how important the Torah is to Jews.

Once, I was walking along the road when a certain man met me. He greeted me and I returned his greeting. He said to me, "Rabbi, where are you from?" I said to him, "I am from a great city of scholars and scribes." He said to me, "Rabbi, if you would be willing to live with us in our place, I will give you a thousand thousand gold coins, as well as precious stones and pearls." I said to him, "Even if you give me all the silver and gold and precious stones and pearls in the world, I would not live anywhere else but in a place where the people study the Torah. At the time when a man dies, neither silver nor gold nor precious stones nor pearls accompany him—nothing except the Torah he has studied and the good deeds he has performed."

*From "The Sayings of the Fathers,"
Chapter 6 paragraph 9*

WORSHIP IN THE SYNAGOGUE

This section tells you about how Jews worship in the synagogue.

For Jews, worship means praying to God, thanking him for the things he has done, and asking for his help in their lives. They believe that worshiping God is very important.

Jews do not believe that they can only worship God if they are in the synagogue. They worship him in other places too. But every **Shabbat**, the Jewish holy day, many Jews go to the synagogue because it is a special place to worship

God. As they go into the synagogue, some Jews wash their hands. This is not because they are dirty; it is a symbol to make them fit for prayer. Then they say a prayer to thank God for the fact that they can worship him.

A synagogue service includes readings from the Scriptures, prayers, and singing of **psalms**. (A psalm is a kind of poem.) Usually there is a talk called a **sermon**. Some synagogue services include readings from the Torah, the Books of Teaching that are written on scrolls. The scrolls are carried carefully from the Ark to the bimah to be read, and back again after the reading is finished. For a full synagogue service to be held

This boy is dressed for worship.

in Orthodox Judaism, ten men must be present. (See pages 40–41). If there are not ten men, the service will still be held, but not all of the prayers will be said.

Special clothes

At services in the synagogue, men wear a **yarmulke** or **kippah**. A yarmulke is a skull cap, which is often beautifully embroidered. It is worn as a sign of respect for God. At morning services, they also wear a **tallit**. A tallit is a prayer robe, usually made of silk or wool.

In Orthodox synagogues (see pages 40–41), men wear two small black leather boxes with straps as well as the tallit and kippah. These boxes are called **tefillin**. They contain small pieces of parchment. The parchment has short quotations from the Scriptures written on it. One box is worn in the middle of the forehead. This reminds Jews that they must love God with all their mind. The other is worn on the arm, facing the heart. This reminds Jews to love God with all their heart.

A tefillah (plural tefillin) with its contents.

NEW WORDS

Psalm Kind of poem, used like a hymn.
Sermon Special talk which teaches about religion.
Shabbat Jewish sabbath.
Tallit Prayer robe.
Tefillin Small leather boxes containing quotes from the Scriptures.
Yarmulke or **Kippah** Skull cap.

PRAYER ON ENTERING THE SYNAGOGUE

This is the prayer that Jews say as they enter the synagogue.

And I, due to your great kindness, will come into your house, and, in awe of you, I will worship facing towards your holy Temple. "We will go to the house of God in a crowd." How good are your tents, Jacob, your dwellings, Israel!

And I, due to your great kindness, will come into your house, and, in awe of you, I will worship facing towards your holy Temple.

Lord, I love the dwelling of your house and the place where your glory rests.

And I will worship and bow and bend my knee before the Lord, my maker. And as for me, may my prayer come to you in an acceptable time; God, in your great kindness, answer me with the truth of your salvation.

JEWISH HOLY BOOKS

This section tells you about the Jewish holy books.

The complete Jewish Scriptures are called the **Tanakh**. They are divided into three sections.

- Torah (The books of Teaching)
- Nevi'im (The books of the Prophets)
- Ketuvim (The "writings")

Tanakh is a word made up of the first letters of these three names.

The Torah

The Torah is the most important part of the Scriptures. It contains the books Genesis, Exodus, Leviticus, Numbers, and Deuteronomy. For reading in the synagogue, these books are written on scrolls.

The word "Torah" means teaching. The Torah is a group of books that teach Jews what God is like, and how they should live. They include the stories about the creation of the world and about the first Jews. They also include the mitzvot or commandments about worship, festivals, and the right way to live. Some feel there are 613 mitzvot in the Torah. They are about all parts of life. Some Jews follow them more strictly than others. Some Jews follow them very closely, because they believe that it means they are living their lives in the way that God wants.

Another collection of teaching about how to live is called the **Talmud**. It contains the teachings of **rabbis**, collected together over many years and written down in about 500 CE. The Talmud gives much more detail about the Laws in the Torah and helps to explain them.

Scrolls with their mantles and decorations.

A scroll on the Bimah. (Notice the pointer, that is used when reading it.)

Nevi'im

Nevi'im is a collection of books about the history of the Jewish people. It includes the teachings of the **prophets**. Jews believe that the prophets were men and women who had special powers given by God. This meant that they could tell people how God wanted them to live.

Some parts of Nevi'im are read in synagogue services. They are usually read from an ordinary book, not a scroll. Other parts of Nevi'im are not used in the synagogue, although Jews may read them at home.

Ketuvim, teachings, songs, and psalms

Ketuvim means writings, and most of the books contain stories, teachings, songs, and psalms from Jewish history. The book of Ketuvim that is used most often is the Book of Psalms. A psalm is a special poem, something like a hymn. Psalms are often used in synagogue services.

NEW WORDS

Mitzvot Commandments.
Prophet Someone who tells people what God wants.
Rabbi Jewish teacher.
Talmud Collected teachings of the rabbis.
Tanakh Jewish Scriptures.

LET'S LEARN THE ALEPH-BET!

א **Aleph** – this letter is not sounded

ב With a dot it is **Bet** – pronounced "B"
Without a dot it is **Vet** – pronounced "V"

ג **Gimmel** – pronounced "G" as in "garden"

ד **Dalet** – pronounced "D"

ה **Hey** – pronounced "H"

ו **Vav** – pronounced "V"
With a dot in the center it is
pronounced "OO" as in "hook"
With a dot on top it is
pronounced "AW" as in "saw"

ז **Zayin** – pronounced "Z"

ח **Chet** – pronounced "CH" as in a Scottish "loch"

ט **Tet** – pronounced "T"

י **Yod** – pronounced "Y"

ך כ With a dot it is **Kaph** – pronounced "K"
Without a dot it is **Chaph** –
pronounced "CH" as in a Scottish "loch"

ל **Lamed** – pronounced "L"

ם מ **Mem** – pronounced "M"

ן נ **Nun** – pronounced "N"

ס **Samech** – pronounced "S"

ע **Ayin** – this letter is not sounded

ף פ With a dot it is **Pey** – pronounced "P"
Without a dot it is **Fey** – pronounced "F"

ץ צ **Tsadi** – pronounced "TS" as in "let's"

ק **Kooph** – pronounced "K"

ר **Resh** – pronounced "R"

ש **Shin** – pronounced "SH"

ש **Sin** – pronounced "S"

ת **Tav** – with or without a dot,
pronounced "T" in modern Hebrew

The Hebrew alphabet

SHABBAT

This section tells you about Shabbat, the Jewish day of rest and worship.

Shabbat is the Hebrew word for the Sabbath. It is the Jewish day of rest. It begins at sunset on Friday evening, and lasts until dusk on Saturday.

Shabbat is the oldest of the Jewish holidays. Jews remember the story in the book of Genesis about how God made the world. The story says that God worked for six days, and on the seventh day he rested. So Jews also rest on the seventh day of the week, which is Saturday.

Jews think that the Sabbath is very important. They believe that it is a special gift from God. It is a day of peace and rest. Jews look forward to the Sabbath all week. It is so special that it is welcomed that night as "Sabbath Bride."

Celebrating Shabbat

During Friday, the house is cleaned and the table set, so that everything is ready to welcome the Sabbath. The Sabbath begins at sunset on Friday evening. In order to start the Sabbath celebration, someone lights two candles, and then there is a prayer asking God to bless the home. After several prayers, a blessing for the children is made.

There is always a service in the synagogue on a Friday evening. At some point in the evening there is a Shabbat dinner and a Sabbath service. The Shabbat dinner is the most important meal of the week, and every family tries to make it the best they can afford. It is a relaxed, happy meal when families can enjoy each other's company, and Jews look forward to it from one week to the next.

The table is always covered with a clean white cloth, and the meal begins when the head of the family recites a blessing called the **kiddush** over a cup of wine. Sabbath hymns are sung as the family sits at the table. The Sabbath meal often includes special foods, and there are always two loaves of bread. This is called **challah**, which is specially baked for the Sabbath. A blessing is said over the bread before it is eaten.

Lighting the Shabbat candles. (Notice the challah under its cover.)

The havdalah ceremony, with candle and spice box.

On Sabbath morning, many Jews go to the service at the synagogue. To make the Sabbath different from any other day and to show how important it is, traditional Jews are encouraged to rest completely, and not do any work. Jews who are careful to observe all the ritual laws do not, for example, drive anywhere or go shopping. More liberal Jews are encouraged to enjoy activities that celebrate the spirit of the Sabbath.

The Sabbath ends on Saturday evening, when the father says another blessing called the **havdalah**. A special candle is lit, and everyone smells a special box of spices. The pleasant smell of the spices spreads through the house. Jews hope that this is a symbol of the way the peace and quiet of Shabbat will be remembered all through the coming week. After the blessing, the havdalah candle is put out by dipping it in a cup of wine. Shabbat is over when three stars can be seen in the sky.

NEW WORDS

Challah Special bread for the Sabbath.
Havdalah Blessing that ends the Sabbath.
Kiddush Blessing that begins the Sabbath.

FROM THE KIDDUSH FOR SABBATH

God blessed the seventh day and pronounced it holy, for on it he rested from all the work which he had created to set the Universe in motion.

You are blessed, Lord our God, King of the Universe, who creates the fruit of the vine.

You are blessed, Lord our God, King of the Universe, who has made us holy with his commandments and has desired us and who, with love and goodwill, has made us inherit his holy Sabbath—a remembrance of the work of creation. For it is a day which is the beginning of all holy celebrations, a remembrance of the departure from Egypt. For you have chosen us and sanctified us from among all nations, and you have made us inherit your holy Sabbath in love and goodwill. You are blessed, Lord, who makes the Sabbath holy.

ROSH HASHANAH AND YOM KIPPUR

This section tells you about the important days at the time of the Jewish New Year.

Rosh Hashanah

Rosh Hashanah is the Jewish New Year. Jews have their own calendar, so New Year is not on January 1. It falls in late September or early October. Jewish years are also numbered in a different way. They are 3761 years ahead of the Gregorian, or Western, calendar that is used in most countries. For example, the Jewish year 5756 began in autumn 1995, the year 5761 will begin in 2000, and so on.

Rosh Hashanah reminds the Jews how God made the world. It is also the beginning of the most solemn time of the year. This lasts for ten days, which are called the Days of Returning. In these ten days, Jews think about the things they have done wrong in the past year. They make promises to themselves and to God that they will do better in the future.

The night before Rosh Hashanah, Jews have a meal at home. A special part of the meal is eating apples dipped in honey. This is a way of saying that everyone wishes that the year that is beginning will be sweet and pleasant.

A special synagogue service is held at Rosh Hashanah. The **shofar** is blown. A shofar is a ram's horn, hollowed out so that notes can be played on it. The notes it plays sound very solemn. They remind the people that God is very powerful, and they must listen to him.

Yom Kippur

Yom Kippur comes at the end of the Days of Returning. It is the Day of **Atonement**, which is the most solemn day of the year. Atonement means making up for something you have done wrong. It is a day when Jews pray to God to forgive them for the things they have done wrong.

Eating apples and honey

16

Blowing the shofar.

At Yom Kippur, Jews **fast** for 25 hours. (This means they go without any food or drink.) They spend a lot of the day at the synagogue. They believe that if they are really sorry for the wrong things they have done God will forgive them. As well as praying for forgiveness, Yom Kippur is a day for remembering how kind God is, and how much he loves them. In the synagogue, the Ark and the reading desk are covered in white cloths, and the people leading the service wear white, too. This is a symbol to show that God has taken away the sins of the people who are sorry for what they have done wrong.

At the end of the service, the shofar is blown again. Its meaning is different from when it was blown at Rosh Hashanah. This time it reminds people that they must remember all the good things they have promised to do, and live good lives throughout the coming year.

NEW WORDS

Atonement Making up for something you have done wrong.
Fast Go without food and drink, often for religious reasons.
Shofar Ram's horn instrument.

PRAYER FOR THE DAYS OF RETURNING

This is part of a prayer used in Reform synagogues during the Days of Returning. (See pages 40–41.)

The old year has died and the new year has scarcely begun. In this pause before the account is made of the past and my life is judged for what it is, I ask for honesty, vision, and courage. Honesty to see myself as I am, vision to see myself as I should be, and the courage to change and realize myself.

Your hand is open to every living being. At the smallest sign you come to meet us, for you are generous to forgive. On this day of repentance and return, stretch out your hand to me, so that I may grasp it, and lead me along the paths of love and duty into the harmony and peace which you have prepared for me.

SUKKOT

This section tells you about Sukkot, the Feast of **Tabernacles**.

Tabernacle is an old word that means a type of tent. The Hebrew word for this tent or hut is **sukkah** (plural sukkot). The Feast of Tabernacles is the next major festival of the Jewish year. In Hebrew it is called Sukkot. The festival lasts a week. Some Jews build a sukkah in the garden, and live or eat in it for the week. The temple usually builds a sukkah.

The Feast of Tabernacles celebrates two things.

- It recalls how the Jews in old days used to take offerings of fruit to the Temple.

- It recalls how the Jews were once traveling in the desert and lived in tabernacles.

A sukkah.

The most important part of the sukkah is the roof. This is made of branches and has fruit hung from it. It is built so that the sky can be seen through it. This is a reminder of the time in Jewish history when Jews were traveling in the desert with no real home.

Carrying the lulav and citron.

At the special synagogue service, everyone holds branches of certain trees. These are called the "lulav." The trees are palm, willow, and myrtle. The people hold the branches in their right hands. In their left hands they each hold a citron or "etrog." A citron is a yellow fruit something like a lemon. During the service, the people walk around the synagogue carrying these things. They also wave the branches. They are waved in all directions to show that God rules all the universe.

Each of the things they carry has a meaning. A sign or object that has a special meaning is called a symbol. The palm symbolizes the spine. The willow symbolizes the lips. The myrtle symbolizes the eyes. The citron symbolizes the heart. Joining them together reminds Jews that God must be worshiped with every part of them.

Simchat Torah

The day after the end of the Feast of Tabernacles is called Simchat Torah. This means the Rejoicing of the Torah. The books of the Torah are Genesis, Exodus, Leviticus, Numbers, and Deuteronomy. They are very important for Jews. Parts of the books are read every week in services in the synagogue. During the year, the five books are read all through. At Simchat Torah, there is a special ceremony when the last part of the book of Deuteronomy is read, followed by the first part of the book of Genesis. Jews believe that the books show the way God wants them to live, so reading them like this is a way of showing that they should never stop following what God wants.

Simchat Torah is a very happy day. All the scrolls are taken out of the Ark and carried around the synagogue with the people dancing, singing, and clapping after them. To celebrate the festival, children in the synagogue are given bags of candies and fruit.

NEW WORDS

Sukkah Hebrew word for tabernacle.
Tabernacle A type of tent.

HOW A SCROLL IS MADE

A scroll is made of parchment, which is a special writing material made from animal skins. For a scroll, the animal must be kosher. (See pages 42–43.) The parchment is made in sheets that are stitched together. Traditionally, the threads used for stitching were tendons from the feet of a kosher animal. The ends are stitched around a wooden roller called the Etz Hayim, which means tree of life. The rollers are used to wind the scroll to the part that is to be read.

The writing on a scroll is in columns. A full Torah scroll has 250 columns. The writing is done by specially trained scribes, who write with special black ink using a quill pen made from the feather of a kosher bird. The writing must be perfect. If the scribe makes a mistake in a normal word, it can be rubbed out with a pumice stone, but if he makes a mistake in a word that refers to God, the piece of parchment must be carefully cut out and buried. (There are places in Jewish graveyards for this.) A patch is then stuck under the hole and pressed down so that the word can be rewritten. It takes a scribe about 1,000 hours to complete a full Torah scroll.

HANUKKAH

This section tells you about the festival of Hanukkah.

Hanukkah is a winter festival. It usually falls in December, and it lasts for eight days. It is sometimes called the Festival of Lights.

The story of Hanukkah

Hanukkah reminds the Jews of events that happened over two thousand years ago. It celebrates the bravery of a small group of Jews who were led by a man called Judah. His nickname was "the hammer." In Hebrew, hammer is "maccabee," so he is called Judah the Maccabee.

Lighting the Hanukkiah or the Hanukkah menorah.

Judah was the leader of a small group of men who were fighting for what they believed. Their country had been taken over by an enemy. The new ruler was called Antiochus. He would not let the Jews worship their own God. He said that they had to worship him! The Jews knew that Antiochus was only a man, and it would be wrong to worship him.

Judah and his small group of friends fought against the cruel emperor Antiochus for three years. At last they managed to beat his army in a battle. The battle was important because it meant that they had captured Jerusalem. Jerusalem is a very important city for the Jews. The Temple was in Jerusalem, and the Temple was the most important building in the Jewish religion. Antiochus had tried to spoil the Temple, so that Jews could not use it. He had ordered that a pig should be killed on the altar, one of the most important parts of the Temple. This made the Temple unclean— far worse than just dirty. It could not be used to worship God again until it had been specially cleaned and made holy again.

After Judah had captured Jerusalem, one of the first things he did was give orders that the Temple should be made ready for worship again. When the Temple was ready, the menorah was lit. This was the Temple lamp, which had seven branches. The menorah was supposed to burn all the time, but Antiochus had let it go out. When it was lit again, Judah's men discovered that it only had enough oil in it to burn for one night. They went to get more oil, but the oil was special, and it took eight days to get it. When the soldiers got back, the lamp was still lit. The people said that this was a **miracle**. God had made the lamp burn even though it did not have enough oil. This showed that God was pleased that the Temple had been made ready for worship again.

Playing the dreidel game.

Celebrating Hanukkah

When they celebrate the festival today, Jews use a special branched candlestick in their homes. It is called a **Hanukkiah.** It is a candlestick with eight branches and an extra holder for the "servant candle" that is used to light all the others. One candle is lit on the first night of the festival, two on the second night, and so on. Each one is lit using the ninth candle. Before each candle is lit, special prayers are said. By the end of the festival, all nine candles are burning. Some Jews burn olive oil instead of candles, so that it is more like the miracle in the Temple.

Hanukkah is a very happy festival, especially for children. They go to parties and give each other presents. There is a special game that children play at Hanukkah using a four-sided top called a **dreidel**. On each side of the dreidel there is a Hebrew letter. The letters are the first letters of the Hebrew words that say "A great miracle happened here."

NEW WORDS
Hanukkiah A nine-branched Hanukkah menorah.
Dreidel Four-sided top.
Miracle Event that cannot be explained.

HOW TO PLAY THE DREIDEL GAME

- Make or buy a four-sided spinning top.

- On each side, paint one of the Hebrew letters.

Nun נ   Hey ה

Gimmel ג   Shin ש

- Have ready a "bank" of candies, nuts, or counters in the middle of the table.

- Spin the dreidel.
  - If Nun comes up, this means you take nothing.
  - If Hey comes up, you take half of the candies.
  - If Gimmel comes up, you take all the candies.
  - If Shin comes up, you put the candies back into the bank.

- The game goes on with players adding to the bank if it empties, until a player taking all the candies is declared the winner.

PURIM

This section tells you about the festival of Purim.

Purim is a very exciting festival, especially for children. It takes place in February or March. Purim tells the story of a good queen and a bad man. The story is in the Jewish Scriptures and in the Bible. It is called the Book of Esther.

The story of Purim

Esther was the name of the good queen. The bad man was called Haman. They lived a long time ago in a country called Persia. Haman was the King's Chief Minister in the government. He had quarreled with a Jew who refused to bow as Haman passed. Bowing is a sign of worship, and Jews believe that it is wrong to worship anyone except God. Haman disliked the Jews, and, because he was so angry, he made a plan to kill all the Jews in Persia. To do this, he had to get the king to order the killings. Haman went to the king and told lies about the Jews. The king agreed that all Jews in the country should be killed. Haman could not make up his mind on which day the killings should be carried out, so he decided to draw lots. *Purim* is a word for "lots," and this gives the festival its name.

Queen Esther heard about this. Although the king did not know it, she was Jewish. She decided that the Jews must be saved. The only way this could happen was if she could persuade her husband, the king, to change his

A play for Purim.

This scroll of the Book of Esther is in the Jewish Museum in London.

...nind. This was a dangerous thing to try to do— she was only supposed to go to see the king when he sent for her! She was very brave. She invited the king and Haman to a feast. During the meal she told her husband the real reason why Haman wanted to kill all the Jews. The king was very angry. He ordered that Haman should be killed, and all the Jews were saved.

Celebrating Purim

At the Festival of Purim, the story of how all this happened is read out in the synagogue. Every time the children hear the name of Haman, they make as much noise as they possibly can. They stamp their feet. They use special rattles (called **gragers**) and whistles. The idea is to make so much noise that Haman's name cannot be heard at all.

At Purim, children often go to formal parties. Sometimes they put on special plays at school or in the synagogue to show the story. In Israel there are plays and carnivals in the streets. Purim is also a time when Jews give money to charity, and give gifts of food to each other. This makes sure that even poor people can celebrate the festival with a special meal.

NEW WORD

Grager Rattle used by children at Purim.

HAMANTASCHEN

Hamantaschen—"Haman's purses"— are a traditional food at Purim.

Pastry	*Filling*
12 oz. plain flour	2 tablespoons milk
4 oz. sugar	2 tablespoons honey
1 teaspoon baking powder	2 oz. sugar
1 egg, beaten	4 oz. poppyseeds
4 oz. margarine, creamed	2 oz. walnuts
2 tablespoons orange juice	1 teaspoon lemon juice
	grated rind of $\frac{1}{2}$ a lemon

Make the pastry: Sift together the flour, sugar, and baking powder. Mix the egg, margarine, and juice. Add the two mixtures together. Refrigerate for several hours. Roll out to $\frac{1}{12}$ inch (2 mm) thickness, and use a $\frac{1}{4}$ inch (6 mm) cutter to cut into circles.

Make the filling: Boil the milk, honey, and sugar together. Add poppyseeds and cook for 5 minutes. Add remaining ingredients and cook until mixture thickens.

Make the Hamantaschen: Cool filling and then put $\frac{1}{2}$ teaspoon of filling in the center of each round. Pinch the pastry together to make triangle "purses." Preheat the oven to 350°F (180°C), place the pastries on a greased baking tray, and cook for 10–12 minutes until golden. Cool on a wire tray.

PESACH

This section tells you about the story of Pesach, the Feast of Passover.

Passover is perhaps the most popular Jewish festival. It celebrates something that happened over 3,000 years ago. In those days, the Jews were living in Egypt. The king of Egypt was called the **Pharaoh**. The Pharaoh had made the Jews slaves. Their lives were very difficult. They had to work very hard and were very badly treated. They had to build enormous storehouses for the Pharaoh. He had special slave drivers to make them work hard. If they did not work fast enough, or if the slave drivers felt like it, they were beaten with whips.

One of the Jews was a man called Moses. God spoke to Moses, telling him that he was to rescue the Jews. He went to the Pharaoh and said, "Let my people go!" The Pharaoh refused, but then a series of disasters happened in Egypt. They are called **plagues**. Everyone believed that these plagues had been sent by God. Flies, frogs, locusts, cows dying … altogether there were ten plagues. Each time there was a plague the Pharaoh said that the Jews could go. As soon as the plague ended, he changed his mind and said that they must stay. The last plague was the most terrible. The eldest son in each Egyptian family died. God warned Moses that this would happen. He told Moses to tell the Jews to put lambs' blood on the doorjambs of their houses. Then Jewish boys would not die.

The ten plagues.

Hail

Locusts

Boils

Death of the eldest son

Frogs

Rivers turned to blood

Darkness

Flies

Lice

Death of cattle

The Pharaoh was so upset by the death of the boys that he said the Jews really could go. They prepared to leave as quickly as they could. They needed food for the journey, but there was no time to wait for the yeast to rise in the bread that they made. It was baked as it was. Although he had said they could leave, the Pharaoh changed his mind again. He sent his army after the Jews to bring them back. They were saved because of the water in the Sea of Reeds. It parted to allow them to cross. As soon as the Egyptian army tried to follow them, the sea flooded back and the Egyptians were drowned.

Passover reminds the Jews of three things.

- God is good—he helped his people.

- Death "passed over" the houses of the Jews.

- The Jews passed through the Sea of Reeds (probably the north end of the Red Sea) when they were leaving Egypt.

One of the plagues was a swarm of locusts.

NEW WORDS

Pharaoh King of Egypt.

Plague Disaster sent by God.

KEEPING THE PASSOVER

This quotation from the Book of Exodus tells how Moses told the Jews to keep the Passover.

Remember this day as the time when you departed from Egypt, from the house of slavery, when the Lord took you out of here with his great power — nothing leavened may be eaten. For seven days you shall eat matzo, and the seventh day will be a festival for the Lord. Matzo must be eaten for the seven days and neither anything leavened nor any yeast must be seen in your possession throughout all your territories. And on that day you must explain to your children why you are doing this, saying to them, "The Lord did wonders for me when I went out of Egypt so that I could carry out these commandments." And the commandments shall be written as a sign bound onto your hand and a memorial placed on your forehead, so that the Torah of the Lord should become part of your everyday conversation, for the Lord brought you out of Egypt with his great power. And you must observe this practice at its proper time, year by year.

Exodus 13 : 3, 6–10

CELEBRATING PESACH

This section tells you how Jews celebrate Pesach, the Feast of Passover.

Passover takes place in late spring. Before the festival begins, the house is cleaned. Any **leaven** is removed. Leaven is anything like baking powder or yeast that makes dough rise. This is a reminder that when the Jews were leaving Egypt there was no time for the bread to rise. On the night before the festival begins, the house is searched. Any tiny piece or crumb of leaven is swept up with a feather and burned. Nothing that contains leaven is eaten during the festival.

The Seder

The main part of the Passover celebration is a meal. This is called the **Seder**. The Seder meal follows a special order that is written down in a book called the **Haggadah**. The Haggadah tells the story of the slavery and how the Jews left Egypt. The story is told as the meal is eaten. The youngest child present at the meal asks four questions. The questions are answered as the family reads the story. In the answers to the questions, the person leading the meal talks about the things on the Seder plate. This is a special plate divided into five sections. Each section contains a special food. The foods are symbols that remind the Jews of the slavery and how they left Egypt.

Special foods for the Seder

- Shank bone—not eaten, but a reminder of the lamb that was killed so its blood could be put on the doorjambs.

- Egg—hard-boiled, then roasted in a flame. A reminder of the animals that used to be **sacrificed** in the Temple, and a symbol of new life.

- Green vegetable—usually parsley or lettuce. A symbol of the way God cared for the Jews when they were traveling in the desert.

- Bitter herbs—usually horseradish. A symbol of the bitterness of slavery.

- Charoset—a sweet mixture of apples, nuts, spices, and wine. A reminder of the cement used by the slaves when they were building, and a symbol of the sweetness of freedom.

There are three other important things on the table.

The Seder meal.

The Seder plate with matzo.

- A bowl of saltwater, which is a symbol of the tears of the slaves. The parsley or lettuce is dipped in this.

- A glass of wine for each person. Wine is drunk four times during the meal. This is a reminder of the four promises that God made to Moses.

- **Matzo**, which are flat crackers or pieces of unleavened bread. These are a reminder of the bread that did not rise.

Not everything eaten at Passover has a meaning. The Seder also includes a real meal. At the end of the Seder, the family stays at the table and sings songs. Many have repeated words or phrases that even very young children can enjoy joining in.

Passover reminds Jews of their history and of how Jews have suffered more recently. It helps them to look forward to a time of peace and joy. The last words of the Seder are:

Next year in Jerusalem,
Next year may all be free.

NEW WORDS

Haggadah Book the Seder is written in.
Leaven Yeast, baking powder, etc.
Matzo Unleavened bread.
Seder Special Passover meal.
Sacrifice Offering made to a god.

A PASSOVER SONG

Many songs are sung at Passover. This one has been translated to fit the tune of "Green grow the rushes, Oh!"

> *Who knows what one is, now our*
> * Seder's finishing?*
> *I know what one is:*
> *One is God forevermore on earth and*
> *up in heaven.*

The verses count through to thirteen like this.

> *Two are the stones of Law on which*
> * the Cov'nant's given,*
> *Three are the Fathers of the Jews,*
> *Four are the People's mothers,*
> *Five are the books of the Torah,*
> *Six are the sections of Mishnah,*
> *Seven are the days in ev'ry week,*
> *Eight is the day to circumcise,*
> *Nine are the months of pregnancy,*
> *Ten are the commandments,*
> *Eleven are the stars in Joseph's dream,*
> *Twelve are the tribes of Israel,*
> *Thirteen virtues God displays.*

SHAVUOT

This section tells you about Shavuot, the Feast of Pentecost.

The Feast of Pentecost is held seven weeks after the Feast of Passover. This is why it is sometimes called the Feast of Weeks. In Hebrew its name is Shavuot. It celebrates the Jews' belief that God gave the Ten Commandments to Moses.

Before the festival begins, the synagogue is decorated with fruit and flowers. This is often done by the children. It reminds people of how Mount Sinai bloomed with flowers when God came down to give the Torah to Moses.

Celebrating Shavuot

The festival begins with a service in the synagogue. This includes the reading from the Scriptures about how God gave the Ten Commandments to Moses. The Ten Commandments are a set of rules about how to live. Jews believe that they were given to Moses when the Jews were traveling in the desert after they had left Egypt. Jews believe that this is the most important thing that has ever happened to human beings, because it was God telling people how he wanted them to live.

Synagogues are decorated for Shavuot.

Many of the Ten Commandments are quite long, but the rules they give can be summed up like this.

1 I am the Lord your God.

2 You must not have any other gods but me.

3 You must not use God's name carelessly.

4 Remember to keep the Sabbath day holy.

5 Respect your father and your mother.

6 You must not murder.

7 You must not commit **adultery**.

8 You must not steal.

9 You must not tell lies about other people.

10 You must not **covet**.

After the synagogue service, there is a festival meal at home. Part of the meal is two special loaves of bread. They are decorated with a ladder pattern. This reminds Jews of how Moses climbed Mount Sinai to talk to God and was given the Ten Commandments.

Ladder bread.

NEW WORDS

Adultery Sexual relationship outside marriage.
Covet Be jealous of what someone else owns.

RECEIVING THE TEN COMMANDMENTS

This passage tells what happened when God gave the Ten Commandments to Moses.

Now as morning broke on the third day, there was thunder and lightning, and a heavy cloud hanging over the mountain, and the sound of the shofar grew very loud, and all the people who were in the camp trembled. Then Moses led the people out from the camp to meet God; and they positioned themselves at the foot of the mountain. By now, Mount Sinai was full of smoke because the Lord had come down upon it in fire; and its smoke rose up like the smoke of a furnace, and the whole mountain shook terribly. Then the sound of the shofar grew louder and louder; Moses spoke, and God answered him in a powerful voice. So the Lord came down on Mount Sinai, onto the top of the mountain; and the Lord summoned Moses to the top of the mountain, and Moses went up.

Exodus 19 : 16–20

JEWISH HISTORY

This section tells you something about Jewish history.

Jewish history began about 4000 years ago in the part of the world that today we call the Middle East. No one person ever "began" Judaism. The beliefs that became the Jewish faith came about gradually. However, some people were important in making it happen.

One of the most important men was called Abraham. (See pages 32–33.) He was the first to believe that there was only one God. He left his home and went on a long journey, because he believed that was what God wanted him to do. God showed him the way to a new country called Canaan. God promised Abraham that one day his descendants would possess this country. This is the reason it is sometimes called the Promised Land.

After Abraham, the next great leader was a man called Moses. (See pages 34–35.) He lived about 500 years after Abraham. When Moses was alive, the Jews were slaves in Egypt. Moses became their leader and rescued them from slavery. These are the events that are remembered at Passover. After they left Egypt, the Jews lived in the desert for about 40 years. Then they settled back in Canaan again.

Jews lived around that area for hundreds of years, although the country's name and its borders changed many times. For most of the time, they were ruled by kings. One of the most famous kings was David. He lived about 3,000 years ago. When David became king, the country was very small and very poor, and the government was badly organized. David changed all that. He ruled well, and the country became rich and respected.

Other people who played an important part in the history of the country were not part of the government. They were called prophets. A prophet is someone who tells people what God wants. Sometimes they told kings too! Some of the prophets were important people in the country. Others were ordinary men and

Historical map of the Middle East.

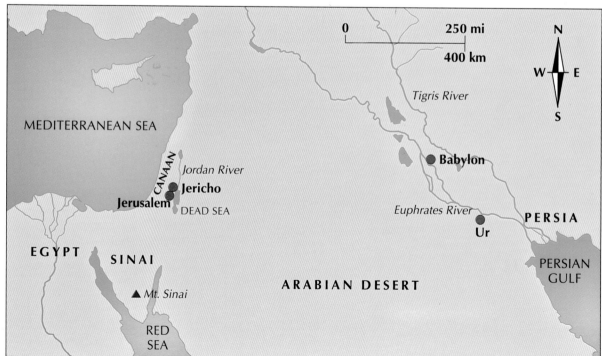

Jews today come from all parts of the world. This boy comes from Ethiopia.

2,600 years ago. He was sure that God wanted him to warn the people that the way they were behaving was wrong. He told them that it would lead to the country being destroyed by an enemy. The people did not like being told this, and Jeremiah was very unpopular. He was put in prison, and people tried to kill him. Even though he did not want to carry on preaching, he felt he had to. He said that God's message was like "a fire burning inside him." His words came true in 598 BCE when Jerusalem was taken over by invaders from a place called Babylon.

During their history, the Jews' country has been taken over several times. Other nations ruled over them. Sometimes Jews were taken away from their own land and made to live in their enemy's country. Other Jews left by choice because they did not want to live being ruled over by their enemies. They went to find a new life somewhere else. This is one of the reasons why today there are Jews all over the world.

women. They all felt that God was telling them what to do and say.

One of the most important prophets was a man called Jeremiah. He lived in Jerusalem about

CHOOSING A PROPHET

This passage tells how God chose the prophet Jeremiah.

And the word of the Lord came to me, as follows,
"Before I formed you in the womb, I knew you,
and before you were born I made you holy—
I have appointed you to be a prophet to the nations."
But I said, "But, Lord God, look, I do not know how to speak, for I am still young."

Then the Lord said to me,
"Do not say 'I am still young,'
for everywhere I send you, you will go,
and everything I command you, you shall speak.
Do not be afraid, for I am with you to take care of you."

Jeremiah 1 : 4–8

ABRAHAM

This section tells you about the first founder of Judaism.

Judaism did not suddenly begin. It developed gradually, and came about through many different people. One of the first and most important of these people was a man named Abraham. He is often called one of the fathers of Judaism.

Abraham lived about 4,000 years ago in a town called Ur. Ur was in the part of the world that today we call Iraq. It was a very beautiful city. It had gardens and tall buildings. Abraham was rich and respected. He and his wife Sarah had servants and lots of sheep and camels. In those days, the number of animals someone owned showed how rich they were.

The people of Ur worshiped many gods. There were gods of the sun, the moon, and the stars. Their worship included many things that Abraham began to see were wrong. For example, they were worshiped with human sacrifices. This means that people were killed so that their life could be an offering to the gods. Abraham began to think that there was one God who ruled everything. He was more important than all the other gods. Gradually, Abraham became more and more sure about this "true" God. He also became sure that God did not want to be worshiped in evil ways.

Abraham felt that God was telling him to leave Ur and travel to another country. He and his family set out. They did not know where they were going, but they believed that God would show them the way to go. In those days, people often moved around from place to place because they needed to search for water for their animals. This is called being a **nomad**. Abraham's journey was different because he felt he was being guided by God.

As they traveled, Abraham felt that he was getting to know more about his God. He felt that a

Moon gods in Ur were worshiped in ziggurats like this.

These nomads still live in almost the same way Abraham did.

pecial relationship was beginning. Jews
believe that God promised Abraham that he
would become the father of a great nation. All
his children and their children forever would
have this same special relationship with God.

NEW WORDS

Nomad Person with no fixed home.

INSTRUCTIONS TO ABRAHAM

This is how the Bible describes what God
told Abraham to do.

> *Now the Lord said to Abraham, "Go
> away for your own good—away from
> your country, the place you were born
> and your father's house—to the land
> which I will show you. And I will make
> you a great nation; I will bless you and
> make your name great, and you will
> become a blessing. I will even bless
> those who bless you, and anyone who
> curses you I will curse; and all the
> families of the earth will be blessed
> through you."*

When Abraham reached the place that
God had told him about, God said,

> *"Raise your eyes, and from where you
> are standing, gaze toward the north
> and the south, toward the east and the
> west. For I shall give all the land which
> you see to you and your descendants
> forever. And I will make your descen-
> dants as numerous as the dust of the
> earth; so that if anyone will be able to
> count the dust of the earth, so your
> descendants will be counted."*

Genesis 12 : 1–3; 13 : 14–17

MOSES

This section tells you about Moses.

Moses was the second great leader of the Jews. He lived at a very difficult time in Jewish history. For many years, the Jews had been slaves in Egypt. They were treated with great cruelty by their Egyptian masters. The Egyptians were afraid that the Jews might try to take over the country, so they decided that they must get rid of all Jews in Egypt. As part of this, they ordered that all baby boys should be killed at birth. Moses was not killed because his mother hid him in a basket by the side of the river. He was found by the Pharaoh's daughter. She took him back to the palace and brought him up as if he were her own son.

When Moses grew up, he saw that the Jews were being very badly treated. One day he lost his temper and killed a slave driver who had beaten a Jew to death. Then he had to leave Egypt, or he too would have been killed. He stayed away for several years, but gradually he became sure that God had work for him to do. God spoke to him, telling him to go back and free the Jews from slavery. At first he tried to make excuses to God about not going back, but at last he did. The Pharaoh did not want to let the Jews go, but a series of disasters (plagues) happened in Egypt. Moses told the Pharaoh that these plagues were sent by God, and at last the Pharaoh agreed to free the Jews.

The Jews' troubles were not over even after they had left Egypt. They spent the next 40 years wandering from place to place. They were nomads. These are called the years in the **wilderness**. A wilderness is like a desert where not very much grows. Eventually they found their way to the country called Canaan, and this became their home.

During the years when they were wandering, Moses was the Jews' leader. Jews believe that while they were in the wilderness, God gave Moses the Torah, the Teaching that Jews follow. This Teaching is very important for Jews because it is part of their agreement with God. This agreement is a very serious one. It is called the **Covenant**. God promised that the Jews

This Egyptian painting shows the Jews as slaves.

The life of Moses.

would be his "Chosen People." This does not mean that they would be his favorites. It means that they were chosen to be given extra responsibilities. God would look after them, even guide them, but, in return, the Jews must obey the laws that God gave.

In Jewish history, this is remembered as God's second promise to the Jews. The first promise was to Abraham. God promised that Abraham would be the father of a great nation. The second promise was to Moses. God would take special care of the Jews, if they obeyed his laws.

NEW WORDS

Covenant Solemn agreement.
Wilderness Place that humans have not developed.

THE COVENANT

This passage tells how God told Moses about the Covenant.

And the Lord said to Moses, "Write these words for yourself, for according to these words I have made an agreement with you and with Israel." And he remained there with the Lord for forty days and forty nights; he neither ate bread nor drank water, and he wrote the words of the agreement on stone blocks— ten statements.

Then when Moses came down from Mount Sinai—the two blocks of the testimony being in Moses' hand as he came down from the mountain— Moses did not know that the skin of his face was still shining from when God had spoken to him. And Aaron and all the Israelites looked at Moses, and saw the skin of his face shining, and they were afraid to approach him. But Moses summoned them and taught them all the words which the Lord had spoken to him on Mount Sinai.

Exodus 34 : 27–32

PERSECUTION

This section tells you about how Jews have been punished for their faith.

Persecution means being punished for what you believe. Jews have been among the most persecuted people in history. No one has ever been able to explain why this is so. The most likely reason is that Jews have been misunderstood. For example, Jews believe that they are God's "chosen people." Sometimes non-Jews have thought that this means that Jews feel they are better than other people.

Keeping their own religion and customs is very important for Jews. This has been the only way that their religion has survived. Sometimes this was seen by other people as being dangerous or threatening. It meant that Jews were different, and people are often afraid of what they do not understand. Sometimes, customs were really misunderstood. In other cases, they were deliberately "twisted" so that Jews could be accused of things they had not done. In the Middle Ages, Jews were often persecuted by **Christians** who blamed them for killing Jesus. This was one reason why Jews suffered from persecution in Europe for centuries. During the 1200s and 1300s this was especially harsh.

The most serious persecution of Jews took place in the 1930s and 1940s, when the Nazis were in power in Germany. Their leader was Adolf Hitler, and he hated the Jews. Dislike because of race or religion is called **prejudice**. Hitler was totally prejudiced against Jews, and he set out to destroy them completely. Little by little, all the Jews' rights were taken away. First, all Jews had to register at a local office. Then they were not allowed to go outside unless they were wearing a badge with the Star of David on it, so that they could be recognized in the street. No one was allowed to buy things from Jewish stores. Jews were not allowed to own cars or use buses or trains. Children were not allowed

Jews in Nazi Germany had to wear a Star of David badge.

to go to school. Jews were not allowed to be outside after 9 p.m. . . . The list went on and on. Then the Nazis introduced what they called the "final solution to the Jewish problem." Special camps were organized, and Jews were rounded up like animals. Some were killed at once. Others were starved, not allowed enough clothes, and had their hair shaved off. Torture was common, and every day thousands were sent to the gas chambers.

By the end of World War II, one in every three Jews in the world had been killed. Six million Jews, one and a half million of them children, were dead. This is too many to imagine, but think of it as equal to one in every forty-two people in the United States today.

It is important to ask how this could happen. Most of the people who mistreated the Jews were more or less normal. They acted as they did because Hitler managed to persuade them that Jews were not human. He said they were animals, who were responsible for all the many problems that Germany had at that time. This is called making someone a **scapegoat**—blaming them for something that is not their fault. Many people in Germany were ready to make the

ews scapegoats for all their problems, and so
he Jews were persecuted.

The awful suffering that they have gone
through helps to explain why many Jews today
are very aware of their "Jewishness." It also
explains why family life is so important.

> "First they came for the Jews
> and I did not speak out -
> because I was not a Jew.
> Then they came for the communists
> and I did not speak out -
> because I was not a communist.
> Then they came for the trade
> unionists and I did not speak out -
> because I was not a trade unionist.
>
> "Then they came for me -
> and there was no one left
> to speak out for me."

*These words were written by Pastor Niemoller,
a victim of the Nazis.*

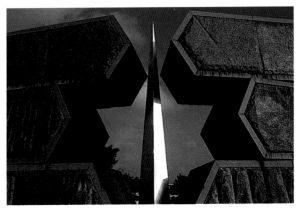

*This sculpture is part of the memorial at Yad
Vashem to Jews killed by the Nazis.*

NEW WORDS

Christian Follower of Jesus.
Persecution Ill-treatment because of
one's beliefs.
Prejudice Unjustified dislike, often
based on race or religion.
Scapegoat Person made to take blame
for others.

ANNE FRANK

Anne Frank was a Jewish girl whose
family went into hiding from the Nazis in
Holland. This is part of what she wrote in
her diary on November 19, 1942.

*Countless friends and acquaintances
have gone to a terrible fate. Evening after
evening, the grey and green army trucks
trundle past. The Germans ring at every
front door and inquire if there are any
Jews living in the house. If there are any,
the whole family has to go at once. If
they don't find any, they go on to the
next house. No one has a chance of
evading them unless they go into hiding.
Often they go around with lists, and only
ring when they know they can get a
good haul. . . . In the evenings when it's
dark, I often see rows of good, innocent
people accompanied by crying children,
walking on and on, in charge of a couple of these guys, bullied, and knocked
about until they almost drop. No one is
spared—old people, babies, expectant
mothers, the sick—each and all join in
the march of death. And all because
they are Jews!*

MODERN JEWISH HISTORY

This section tells you about recent Jewish history.

The Jews' homeland is called Israel. Israel is a Hebrew word that means one who struggles with God. Israel includes more or less the same area of land as Canaan, the country that Jews believe God gave to Abraham.

After World War II, many people in the world felt that Jews should have a country where they would be safe from persecution. Many Jews had gone to live there, and many more were **refugees** who wanted to go there. Israel was finally made a separate country in 1948. The law of Israel says that all Jews have the right to go and live there if they wish.

The Arab countries that are Israel's neighbors were very angry that the land had been given to the Jews. Arabs had lived there for hundreds of years, and they felt that the land should stay Arab. Jews feel that the land is theirs because God promised it to Abraham and Jews lived there long before the first Arab settled there.

Soon after Israel became a separate country, Arab armies attacked it because their leaders thought that the state should not be allowed to exist. There were major wars between Jews and

The Western Wall is an important place of pilgrimage.

The position of Israel.

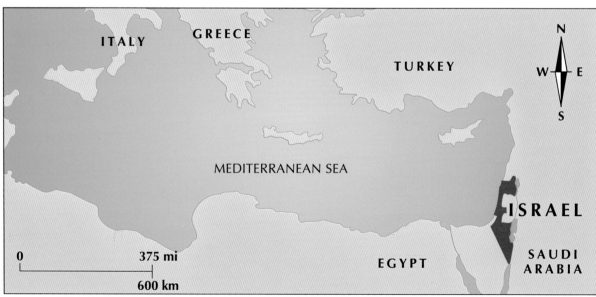

Arabs in 1956, 1967, and 1973. For years the two sides could not agree. But, in 1978, the Camp David Accords were agreed on by Israel and Egypt. There are still many problems along the borders of Israel. Syria, for example, and Israel have areas of land that they both claim should belong to them.

There has been tremendous discord in recent years. The Palestinian uprisings and hopes for an independent nation are only one side of this painful story. Israeli leaders of great stature, including Yitzhak Rabin, have helped the peace process along. Mr. Rabin was speaking for peace just moments before he was assassinated by an Israeli extremist who was against peace. Great leaders, like former Prime Minister Rabin, have made proposals and have come to the peace table along with Yasir Arafat, the Palestinian leader, and King Hussein of Jordan. Gaza and parts of the West Bank have been returned to Palestinian control. The world is still hoping for true peace in the area.

The Western Wall is all that remains of the Temple that was destroyed by Romans in 70 CE. In its place stands an important mosque—a place of **pilgrimage** for **Muslims.**

This model shows what the Temple in Jerusalem looked like.

NEW WORDS

Muslim Follower of the religion of Islam.
Pilgrimage Journey made for religious reasons.
Refugee Person who leaves their country to avoid persecution or danger.

ISRAEL'S DECLARATION OF INDEPENDENCE

This is part of the Declaration of Independence of the State of Israel. It was read out on May 14, 1948.

We, the members of the National Council, representing the Jewish people in the Land of Israel, do hereby proclaim the establishment of a Jewish State in the Land of Israel.

The State of Israel will be open to Jewish immigration and the ingathering of exiles. It will devote itself to developing the land for the good of all its inhabitants. It will rest upon the foundations of liberty, justice, and peace as envisioned by the prophets of Israel. It will maintain complete equality of social and political rights for all its citizens, without distinction of creed, race, or sex. It will guarantee freedom of religion and conscience, of language, education, and culture. It will safeguard the Holy Place of all religions. It will be loyal to the principles of the United Nations Charter.

JUDAISM TODAY

This section tells you about Jewish groups in the world today.

All followers of all religions are individuals, and of course they do not all have the same ideas about their beliefs. Some people may think that one part of the religion is more important than another, and so on. Followers of Judaism all share belief in its basic teachings, but different groups of Jews do not agree about other parts of the religion and about how they should live their lives.

The main groups of Jews in the world today are Orthodox, Reform, and Conservative Jews. In the United States about 7 percent of the Jewish population is Orthodox, 40 percent is Conservative, and 41 percent is Reform.

Orthodox Jews studying the scriptures.

Orthodox Jews

Orthodox Jews believe that traditional ways of observing their religion are important. They keep the traditional laws of Judaism more strictly than other Jews. They believe that the Torah is the word of God, and shows how God wants people to live. The Torah will never

Inside a Reform synagogue.

change, although, as times change, the teachings may be applied in different ways, so that people can know what God wants whenever and wherever they live.

Reform Jews

Reform Judaism, which is about 200 years old, believes that Judaism can change to fit different circumstances. Among the most dramatic reforms are full rights given to women (including the right to be ordained as a rabbi), changing some of the traditional prayers, and affirming that each individual has the right to make personal decisions about how he or she behaves as a Jew.

Conservative Jews

Conservative Judaism was founded in the late nineteenth century as a middle ground between Orthodoxy and Reform. Most important in its philosophy is that Jewish law is still binding, but that major changes can be made in response to the modern world. (Reform Judaism no longer abides by the philosophy that Jewish law is still binding.)

The Jewish People

In spite of the many differences between Jews, they are still united by their common past. Over thousands of years, they have shared a sense of destiny, too. Jews have always known they were destined to do something. They were chosen to make God known to the world. The principle of "K'lal Yisra'el"—the unity of the Jewish people—is an important reminder that Judaism is more than just a religion. Judaism is a culture and tradition linking millions of Jews worldwide.

NEW WORD

Congregation Group of people meeting for worship.

PSALM 121

This psalm includes statements about God that many Jews accept.

A song for the choir standing on the temple stairs

I will lift up my eyes to the mountains,
Where will my help come from?
My help will come from the Lord,
who makes heaven and earth.
He will not let your foot slip,
Your Guardian will not doze.
See, the Guardian of Israel

will not doze or sleep.
The Lord is your protector;
the Lord is your shade
on the right hand.
By day the sun will not strike you,
nor the moon by night.
The Lord will guard you from all harm.
He will protect your life.
The Lord will protect your comings
   and goings
from now and forevermore.

Judaism in the Home

This section tells you something about how Jews keep their religion at home.

Judaism is not just a set of beliefs, but a way of life. The way Jews dress, eat, and live are important parts of following their religion. This section looks at two of many different ways that Jews carry out their beliefs at home. Orthodox Jews are normally much more strict about observing these customs.

Mezuzahs

A **mezuzah** is a tiny parchment scroll with the prayer called the Shema written on it. The scroll is protected by a box of wood, plastic, or metal. The box is fastened to the right-hand side of the doorjambs, except the door to the bathroom. On their way in or out of the room, strict Jews touch the box. It reminds them that God is present in the house.

A scribe writing a mezuzah scroll.

Food

Judaism has laws about what foods may be eaten, and how food should be prepared. Strict Jews keep these laws very carefully. Most Jews keep at least some of the laws. Jewish food stores and many supermarkets sell food that is prepared in keeping with the food laws.

Food that Jews are allowed to eat is called **kosher**. All plants are kosher, but not all fish and animals are. The list of foods that are allowed is in the book of Leviticus. Animals that chew the cud and have split hooves (for example, cows and sheep) are kosher. Animals that do not chew their cud or have split hooves (pigs and rabbits) are not kosher. Fish are allowed if they have fins and scales, but shellfish are not. Any animal to be eaten must be killed in a special way. Before being cooked, the meat is soaked in cold water and sprinkled with salt. This removes all the blood from it. A kosher butcher may prepare the meat so that it is ready for cooking.

The laws say that meat and dairy foods cannot be eaten together. So for example, butter will

A mezuzah.

NEW WORDS

Kosher "Fit"—food that Jews can eat.
Mezuzah Tiny scroll of the Shema.

BIRKAT HAMAZON

This is the beginning of the prayer that is said after meals. Birkat hamazon means "blessings for food."

You are blessed, Lord our God, King of the Universe, who feeds the whole world with your goodness, with grace, kindness, and compassion. He gives food to all living things, for his kindness, is eternal. And in his great goodness food has never failed us, nor will it fail us forever, for the sake of his great name. For he feeds us and sustains everything and does good with every being, and prepares food for all his creatures which he has created. You are blessed, Lord, who provides food for all.

...e foods on the left are kosher, those on the ...ht are not.

...t be used in a meat sandwich, and milk or ...eam sauces will not be eaten with meat.

...ws usually wait at least three hours before ...ixing meat and milk, so a dessert with cus-...rd or cream, or coffee with milk, would not ...low a meat course. To keep meat and milk ...tally separate, many Jewish kitchens have ...o sets of dishes, cutlery, and tablecloths. ...ey also have two sinks, so that the two sets ...n be washed separately.

...r Jews, preparing food carefully and eating it ...e ways of worshiping God, because God has ...ven the food. For the same reason, they thank ...n before and after meals.

SPECIAL OCCASIONS 1

This section tells you about the special things that happen to Jewish children.

Babies

Jewish babies are always given a special Hebrew name, which is often chosen to remember a relation. This name is used as well as their given name, and it will always be used at important religious ceremonies.

Circumcision

Healthy Jewish baby boys are **circumcised** on the eighth day after birth. (If a baby is ill, he will not be circumcised until he is well.) Circumcision means removing the foreskin, the flap of skin at the end of the penis. It is a very common operation. Circumcision may be done by a doctor, or by a rabbi who is specially trained. A boy is given his name during this ceremony, which often takes place after morning prayers at the synagogue. Baby girls are given their names in the synagogue on the Sabbath after their birth.

Bar Mitzvah

A Jewish boy becomes a Bar Mitzvah at the age of thirteen. Bar Mitzvah means "son of the commandments." On the Sabbath after his thirteenth birthday, a boy recites the blessing of the Torah before it is read in the synagogue.

A Bar Mitzvah ceremony in a synagogue in Jerusalem

his Bat Mitzvah girl is holding a copy of the
criptures that she has decorated.

me boys may read the passage from the
orah, too. He must have practiced the Hebrew
ell enough to be able to read it in public.
iends and relatives come to the service, and
ten there may be a celebration meal.

nce he has reached the age of Bar Mitzvah, a
wish boy is counted as a man. He can be one
the ten men necessary before a synagogue
rvice can be held, and he is expected to obey
l the Jewish laws.

at Mitzvah

girl becomes a Bat Mitzvah automatically at
e age of twelve. Bat Mitzvah mean "daughter
the commandments." Not all Orthodox syna-
gues have special services to celebrate Bat
itzvahs. If they do, they are held on a Sunday
ther than the Sabbath. Girls do not read from
e Torah in an Orthodox synagogue. In most
onservative synagogues, girls do read from
e Torah. In a Reform synagogue, there is no
fference between the services held for boys
d girls. A party for family and friends is usu-
ly held after the service.

NEW WORD

Circumcision Removal of the foreskin.

A PRAYER FOR BAR MITZVAH

This is part of the prayer that a boy
says at his Bar Mitzvah in a Reform
synagogue.

*May I be a true Bar Mitzvah, son of
the commandments, taking my place
in the community of Israel, accepting
its responsibilities, rejoicing in its
blessing. May I be a witness to the
living God and his goodness, and
the tradition that lives within me.*

*I remember all those who have
helped me to reach this time. I give
thanks for the love and care of my
family, the patience and instruction
of my teachers, and the support and
companionship of my friends.*

*In the Torah I have read the word of
God. With your help may I go on to
fulfill it in my life. Amen.*

Special Occasions II

This section tells you about what happens at special events in a Jew's life.

Marriage

Judaism teaches that it is important to be married. Usually, a Jew is expected to marry a Jew because it is thought that it will be difficult to keep the tradition going with someone of another faith. A Jewish wedding is conducted by a rabbi, often in a synagogue. The bride and groom always stand under a special canopy called a **huppah.**

During the ceremony the couple will drink from a glass of wine over which a blessing will be said. The "ketubah," a marriage contract binding the husband and wife together, is read publically during the ceremony. At the end of the service, the groom crushes a glass under his foot. This tradition is performed as a reminder that, despite the joy of the wedding, the bride and groom are part of the Jewish people and should not forget the difficult times that Jews have so often been forced to endure. It is also a reminder that the Temple in Jerusalem, the holiest place for Jews, was destroyed.

Divorce

Jews allow couples to divorce, but there are usually great efforts to save a marriage. Friend

The bride and groom stand under the huppa

wish graves.

NEW WORDS

Cremation Burning a body after death.
Huppah canopy used for wedding
ceremony.

d relatives will do their best to help the
uple to solve their problems. If divorce
nnot be avoided, the husband gives the wife
certificate of divorce. This is the only way a
wish marriage can be ended. Jewish law then
lows a person to remarry. (Orthodox Jews
nnot remarry unless they have been granted
religious divorce.)

eath

ws believe that funerals should take place as
on as possible after someone has died. If
ssible, it should be within 24 hours. Funeral
rvices are always very simple. Jews believe
at there should be no difference between rich
d poor, because death happens to everyone.
ne "Kaddish," a prayer praising God, is said
a funeral. After funeral services, the family
serves a period of deep mourning for seven
ys. Most Jews do not allow bodies to be
emated, because they think that it destroys
hat God has made.

fter death

ws do believe in a life after death, but it is not
very important part of their faith. They
lieve that it is more important to concentrate
this life, rather than think about what might
ppen in a future life.

PSALM 100

This psalm is read at Jewish weddings.

A psalm of thanksgiving

Shout out to the Lord, all the earth!
Serve the Lord in happiness!
Come before him with shouts of joy!
Know that the Lord is God.
He made us, and we are his—
his people and the sheep of his
pasture.
Come into his gates with
thanksgiving,
into his courtyards with praises!
Thank him, bless his name.
For the Lord is good
and his kindness is eternal;
and his faithfulness is from
generation to generation.

INDEX

The numbers in **bold** tell where the main definition of the words are.

© 1995 Heinemann Educationa Publishers